A WO
TO PURPOS
FUL

# Becoming Her

**Becoming Her: A Woman's Path to Purpose, Self Love, and Fulfillment**

**Published by CEO Wife Publishing**
www.theceowife.com

The stories in this book reflect each author's recollection of events. Some names, locations, and identifying characteristics have been changed to protect the privacy of those depicted.

Book Creation and Design
Ellese & Co Creative
www.elleseandco.com

ISBN for Paperback: 978-1-7375400-8-3
ISBN for E-book: 978-1-7375400-9-0
Library of Congress Control Number: 2023911466

# DEDICATION

This book is dedicated to the women who fearlessly embark on their journeys of BEcoming! May you find resilience, embrace your power, and bloom into the extraordinary woman you are meant to be.

*Becoming Her*

# Table of Contents

# Foreword
## Precious S. Brown

In our lives, some moments arrive unexpectedly, like gentle whispers or roaring storms, that possess the power to alter our very being. These pivotal moments, where our paths cross, and our destinies take shape, are the threads that weave the pattern of our existence. In these transformative instances, we find the true essence of who we are meant to be.

"Becoming Her" takes readers on a wonderful journey through the lives of women who have encountered pivotal events and felt the call of God. Their experiences epitomize fortitude, bravery, and unflinching resolve. They demonstrate that each of us possesses the capacity to develop, advance, and realize our true potential.

This collection of heartfelt stories is not merely about individual triumphs; it removes all boundaries of gender, race, and background. It represents a testament to the universal human experience—the quest for self-discovery and fulfillment. Through the lens of these women, we witness the unstoppable spirit that resides within each of us, urging us to embrace our unique gifts and rise above the limitations that society may impose.

Each story shares an intense personal transformation. We meet women who have defied societal norms, broken generational cycles, and persistently embraced their passions. They have broken the chains of self-doubt and expectations to move at the beat of their own drum, boldly stepping into their limitless potential. These women embody the audacity to become who they were called to be - divinely.

Through their stories, we gain insight into the often turbulent and exhilarating process of self-discovery. We witness the moments of uncertainty and fear, as well as the moments of bliss and self-realization. These women speak to the resilience that blooms amidst adversity, reminding us that it is in our darkest hours that our true strength is revealed.

As you embark on this fulfillment journey, let the stories within "Becoming Her" inspire you. May they ignite a fire within your soul, urging you to embrace your unique journey and fulfill the divine calling that resonates deep within you. May they remind you that it is never too late to pause and pivot so that you can prosper.

I extend my deepest gratitude to the women whose lives are chronicled within these pages for sharing their experiences, vulnerability, and wisdom. Your journeys inspire us all, a testament to the resilience of the human spirit. Your stories will ignite change, uplift, and empower others who may be on the cusp of their transformation.

Remember, Sunshine, within you lies infinite potential waiting to be unleashed. Embrace the journey of becoming who you were called to be, for it is in your becoming that you illuminate the world with your unique brilliance. And brilliance looks good on you.

With Love,

*Precious S. Brown*

# Shakeasha Shelby

## The Struggle was Real but I Managed to Push Through

# Shakeasha Shelby

## The Struggle was Real but I Managed to Push Thrugh

*"Faith without works is dead"*

*James 2:26*

Sweaty palms and swollen eyes marked the beginning of what I thought would be my 17th Mother's Day without my mother. This one turned out a little differently, though.

My mother came to my great-grandma's house, but while everyone was smiling and opening their Mother's Day gifts, I washed the day away with tears. Knowing that this would be the last day I would cry for her, I stayed in the restroom as long as I could. I told God I couldn't cry for her absence anymore, so I buried her so far in my mind; it was as if I pushed her six feet under myself.

My mom struggled with addiction and I struggled with her absence. Although I was happy to see her, I knew it would be short lived and I couldn't enjoy her the way I wanted to because she would be leaving me again. Even though I felt broken, rejected, abandoned and confused, I always knew I would be alright because of how my grandmother took care of me and my siblings.

But being alright meant me learning to care for myself so I landed my first full-time job at 18 and thought I was all grown. Nobody could tell me anything at that age. I had money and could party with my friends without limits. I thought that was life. I was in school, working, and still living with my grandma, talking about, "I'm grown." When I turned 21, I moved into my place and lived a decent life. I thought I could care for myself and be just fine until I met Ronald.

I was 23 when we met, and I fell hard even though he was younger by about two years. Other girls chased after men with money, but it was all about attention for me. I knew he loved me, and I thought the joy he expressed when I told him I was pregnant three months later proved that he did. I remember thinking it couldn't be true, so I peed on the stick three times to be sure. He was right there when the third result was still positive and so happy; I felt it was the right thing to do to have his child.

Over the next few months, we drifted increasingly apart, and Ronald left me for another woman before our daughter was born. He lied about it for so long and had me believe he wasn't doing anything and that I was trippin'. My gut told me there was another woman. Being six months pregnant and finding out the truth, feeling hurt and alone without anybody to talk to, made me want to take my own life.

I felt I had no reason to live at that point, but I kept pushing through and gave birth to a beautiful baby girl. I never wanted to be a single mother, and what I feared the most came true. Having two mouths to feed made me look at life differently. My perspective changed about how I wanted to live and what I wanted to do with my life. Becoming a mother made me want to attend cosmetology school, so I registered when my little girl was four.

My life was crazy busy. My daughter and I lived independently; I worked full-time and went to school full-time while also trying to be a great mom. I was thankful for my grandmother and my siblings' help because I needed my village's support. I've always been driven and hard-working, so not knowing when to quit has been a major challenge.

Coming home from work one morning and only having two hours of sleep, I fell asleep behind the wheel and hit three parked cars. I was only a couple of blocks away from my house. A young boy woke me by knocking on my car door to see if I was alright. Thanks be to God I was, but I saw I was on the other side of the road and realized my accident could've ended up being so much worse than it was. I knew my life meant more than trying to put Christmas gifts under the tree. I had a life worth living for myself and for my daughter.

After my accident, I took about two months off from school to get myself together. I needed that time to refocus so I could finish what I had started. Instead of returning to school full-time, I put together a part-time schedule. I got the proper rest I needed to better balance my life. I graduated in January 2017 and took my state boards two weeks later.

I failed the written portion but found a job (braiding hair) in a salon. The  owner, Robyn, helped me study for my license, and I retook my license test about a month later. I failed again, this time by only two points. I was so bummed out that I became depressed. I was going to give up. I lost belief in myself that I could pass. Still, I scheduled my retake again and continued studying with Robyn's assistance.

A few weeks later, my grandma was diagnosed with stage three stomach cancer. The news hit me hard, and I felt like shutting down, but I knew I had to pass my boards. I needed my grandma to see me win.

I passed on my third try and couldn't wait to share the news with my grandma. She was so proud even though she wasn't feeling her best. Eventually, God blessed her with a miracle because she overcame her sickness. She beat cancer's butt.

Being a mother gave me strength I didn't even know I had, and I learned how to do it because I was raised by a strong black woman who taught me some things along the way.

My grandma took care of me and my siblings—we were a tribe of about six. Watching her take care of us through struggle and with grace prepared me for motherhood. Being a mother has its challenges, but seeing my baby happy and smiling meant something to me. I knew I would take care of her and love her no matter what. I do for her what my mother couldn't do for me and my siblings.

Immediately after I obtained my cosmetology license, I started my business and worked on building my clientele. I was challenged because I worked as a security guard during the week and did hair on the weekend while still making time to be a mom and a young woman with a social life. Once again, my life was unbalanced. I juggled too many things at once and ran ragged. I knew I needed to quit my job and take the leap in my business.

Instead, my job let me go because I called out for my daughter's birthday, and I dived fearlessly into my business; it was all I had. At this point, I had no choice but to put forth my best effort. My business was my only source of income, but I knew living from paycheck to paycheck wasn't my way of life. I heard "No," a lot when I was growing up, which made me more driven to succeed.

Working has been in me since I was a little girl. I got my work ethic from my grandma; I watched her struggle and rise to become a boss no matter what life threw at her. She always fought back. She was a big role model, and I wanted to work for myself. When I was just 13, I was blessed with my first summer job working as a helper at a daycare. I helped out in the kitchen serving breakfast, snacks, and lunch. I also helped out the director of the daycare with clerical tasks in her office. I only worked for about six weeks but was so happy to buy my school clothes. That was the greatest feeling ever.

Being a boss of myself was always the goal; I just never knew how I would get started. As a little girl, hair has always been of interest to me. I was always seen with a doll or playing with someone else's hair. Of course, I have messed up some heads along the way, but my good and faithful ladies who allowed me to practice my skill helped get me where I am today. They are the real MVPs.

Me and my baby girl have been through some rough times together. We had some challenges, like what happened in September 2019. We were coming home from church on a Thursday evening, and I pulled into the parking structure at my apartment building. For some reason, the clicker that opened the gate wasn't working, so I parked in an outside space. My daughter was only eight years old and sleeping in the back seat. I turned off my car and looked in my rearview mirror. I saw someone wearing a white shirt, and the next thing I knew, a man was at my window pointing a gun at my head. I was shaking and screaming at the top of my lungs.

My screams woke up my daughter, but I didn't want her to scream because it could have made the man point his gun at her. I stopped screaming and prayed to God and Jesus.

I just kept saying, "Jesus, Jesus, Jesus." Something within the man broke.

"I am not like this. I am not like this," he said before telling us to get in the house. He used his gun to drive us away and stood there until we were inside.

I recall him getting into a van that had just pulled up behind my car and driving off. I immediately realized that God had saved me and my daughter. Hours later, we were still so scared that my daughter had to sleep with me to feel safe.

I knew we had to move because our current residence was already unsafe. I was still building my business and felt like I couldn't get a break. I was uncertain of how I would make it work. I needed the first and last month's rent to move. I didn't have it, so we moved in with family.

Even though I knew I only needed assistance for a short time, it felt like a lifetime. We moved in with my grandmother, and although she never did or said anything to make me feel bad, my pride was wounded from having to ask for help. I felt like I wasn't woman enough to care for my family and couldn't support my child. We went back to pinching every penny, and I fell back into depression.

I'd gotten so desperate that I found myself standing outside a blood bank debating whether I should give blood in exchange for gas money. My aunt called to check on me while I was driving back and forth in my car that day. She inquired as to my whereabouts, and when I told her I was considering donating blood in exchange for gas money, I burst into tears. She assured me that all I had to do was ask for her help, but I told her that I didn't want to make my problems her problems.

Thankfully, she gave me the money I needed, and I never went through the door to donate blood.

God was undoubtedly at work in my life. The business was picking up, and after only about two months, I had enough money to relocate. My grandmother did not ask for rent while we were there, which also helped. We found a home through local affordable housing programs, which has been extremely helpful to me over the past few years. Without it, I would have struggled even more, especially since Ronald has never provided much financial assistance.

Being an entrepreneur and a single parent takes courage and is not for the weak. What I've learned along the way is that pivoting can make all the difference. A flexible schedule is also vital to making it all work even when it feels like I can't.

As I write this, the American economy is struggling a bit. I'm pivoting from focusing on doing hair to teaching others how to do hair to help them make ends meet. I've learned to find new lanes to generate revenue. Rebuilding this way is fulfilling because I'm showing girls and young women a way forward. I am proof to not give up on your dreams no matter what life throws at you.

The only person that can block you is the person you see in the mirror. Don't be the person who has a gift but never does anything with it. Become a boss and not a worker. I said that because so many people hate what they do. They wake up and end up drained from living the same routine day in and day out. I couldn't handle being at work for eight hours a day or more and not making what I felt I was worth. I knew I could make more by using my talent and learning new skills. I just had to get out of my own way. My struggles have been the map to my success. Of course, it hasn't been easy, but it has been worth it.

It's easy to apply for a job, get hired, and do what's required. Building a business from the ground up takes work because of the time, money, and effort involved. Every door that closes builds the muscle and confidence you need to succeed.

My business has a consistent clientele, but it took years to get to this point. I generate the revenue I need from my business, and I'm now at a point where I want to show up for young Black and brown girls. I want to show them there's more to life than being a worker, that they can become entrepreneurs and show up more positively than someone else's employee. I show them how they can become whatever they want to be. They only need to find their passion.

I can say God has always had my back and never left me. I know what emotional tears feel like and what healing tears feel like, and they hit differently. When I say, "But God," I mean just that. I smile because I know what grace and mercy look like. I smile because I remain blessed. I smile because I don't look like what I've been through. I smile because I woke up today. I smile because my tomorrow is even better than my yesterday. I smile because God is love. I smile every day because I wake up a better version of myself. I smile because I am walking in my purpose. I smile because I am favored.

Today, I smile because I continue becoming her, the me I am meant to be.

# Dedication

This chapter is dedicated to my daughter, Jayla A. You have encouraged me to be all that I can be and to inspire other black and brown girls around me. You have shown me how to be a better me through your confidence and strength at a very young age.

I love you and because of you is why I am BEcoming - the best version of myself.

# REFLECTIONS

# REFLECTIONS

_____

_____

_____

_____

_____

_____

_____

_____

_____

_____

_____

_____

_____

_____

_____

_____

_____

_____

# Dr. Lashonda Wofford

## Self-Forgiveness:
## Pathway to Freedom

# Dr. Lashonda Wofford

## Self-Forgiveness: Pathway to Freedom

*"Dearly beloved, avenge not yourselves, but rather give place unto wrath: for it is written, Vengeance is mine; I will repay, saith the Lord"*

### *Romans 12:19*

There are so many things we must navigate through this journey called life. Like many, I, too, have been dealt some cards I just wanted to throw back at God.

I say God because that is who I believe to be my higher power. Although I believe in God and trust Him completely, it hasn't always been this way and at times, I was unsure if I could continue trusting and believing in His plan for my life. I questioned Him because I encountered so much pain. It radiated throughout my body to the point that I forgot what it was like to live without pain. My grandmother often said, "You have to forgive because you cannot hold on to unforgiveness" and, "You can't harbor hatred in your heart." She was a woman of great faith and trusted and believed in God and His word. I never saw her faith waiver. She believed with all her heart that God would fix it no matter what she was up against.

Of course, as a child, all of this seemed so easy, but in my early adult life, I learned that trusting and believing in God no matter the situation was not as easy as my grandmother made it look. In my early twenties, I experienced one of the worst things anyone could ever imagine. David, my first husband, was the victim of a violent robbery and was shot multiple times. According to the investigator, nine rounds were fired, and David caught five of them.

His injuries were life-threatening and required me to make tough decisions to save his life. He survived but required around-the-clock care because he was paralyzed from the neck down and needed a ventilator and other mechanical devices to sustain his life. We had a daughter who was only five years old at the time the shooting occurred and very close to her father.

They had a bond that was so beautiful and unbreakable. His love for Shaquandra was unmatched, and he would often talk about how he was a better person because of her.

After months of being in the ICU at the hospital, it was time to decide if David should go to a skilled facility or if I would bring him home and care for him. My heart would not let me send him to a facility for the rest of his life. Against the medical team's advice, I chose to bring him home to live out the rest of his life with me and our daughter.

The prognosis was grim, but I persevered for over seven years. We had nurses in and out of our home 20 hours a day, seven days a week, 365 days a year, to care for almost every need. I provided care when nursing staff was not available.

Approximately two years after David transitioned, our daughter began to act out. She had issues with her grades and just wasn't herself. I didn't understand what was happening because she had always been a good student and a great kid. One day on our ride home from work and school, I talked to her and asked her to explain what was going on with her and why her grades were slipping. Because Shaquandra had never gone to counseling for the trauma she experienced with her dad, I thought maybe she needed to speak to someone about how she was feeling, but she said she was okay, she did not need to speak to anyone, and she would do better.

She cried as she apologized to me for her grades slipping, and I told her we could work through it, but she had to talk to me so I could find the help she needed. After our conversation, I felt bad because I didn't mean to upset her; I just wanted to understand so I could help. A few weeks later, things seemed to be better. Shaquandra received another report card, and sure enough, she had brought all her grades back up. I was so proud of her and ensured she knew it. We celebrated her like never before.

One evening after we were home for the day, I took my shower while Shaquandra was in the kitchen eating and doing her homework. I noticed a handwritten letter on the bed when I got out of the shower. What I read shattered my heart into a million pieces. I could not read the whole letter because the pain that ripped through my chest was breathtaking. My screams filled the house. My daughter ran into my room, and I could not say anything. All I could do was cry and hold my baby.

I tried so many times to speak, but the words just would not come. Finally, I managed to get a few words out.
"Pumpkin, I am so sorry; I had no idea."

I felt like my heart had been snatched from my chest, thrown to the ground, and stomped on. We stayed in my room, holding tight to each other on the floor where she found me. In her letter, my baby explained how she had been sexually abused for years by one of her late father's male nurses. She apologized to me time and time again in her letter for not telling me when it was happening, but she was afraid because he threatened to harm her dad and me if she said anything.

I was so hurt, but that pain quickly turned to rage. That man would die for what he had done to my baby all those years. I promised my daughter that she would never have to worry about him or anyone else violating her again. By this time, I was remarried, so I called my husband and asked him to come home immediately. I called my parents and told them what happened. I asked them if they would come over and watch Pumpkin for a few hours because I needed to do something. They were on their way in minutes. I let my daughter know I had something I needed to do and that her grandparents would watch her until I got back.

Shaquandra knew me very well, and as tears rolled down her face, she begged me not to do anything crazy.

"I need you. I lost my dad and can't lose you, too."

She was terrified of losing me, and as I looked into her eyes, I just could not hurt her any more than she had already been hurt. I promised her I would not blow his brains out like I wanted to. I felt like my hands were tied, but I could do nothing. Reporting him didn't seem like enough; I wanted him gone, completely wiped off the face of the earth.

I did not sleep at all that night. Instead, I cried all night. The next day, we went as a family—my husband, parents, and sister—to the sheriff's department to report my daughter's abuser. This was one of the longest days of my life. While at the sheriff's department, I'm not sure why, but I thought about his wife and kids and became so concerned for them. I told my husband I would call her because she needed to know what her monster of a husband had done to my child.

I immediately got my daughter into counseling, and she continued it until she felt it was no longer serving her. The counselor was very nice, but she couldn't relate to anything my daughter had gone through or was going through. Eventually, we ended formal counseling while continuing to pray to God for healing, guidance, understanding and peace.

The man who assaulted my daughter went to jail for maybe six months. But the most significant part of his sentence is what my daughter wanted more than anything: He had to register as a sex offender for the rest of his life. She wanted to ensure his crime was a public record so people would know what type of animal he was.

How could I let this happen? Why didn't I know that this was happening right under my nose, under my roof? As a mother, our primary job is protecting our children, and I failed. I never wanted to harm myself, but I did want to just lay down, sleep, and never wake up. There was so much to process, and I did not know where to start. All I could do was cry. There were so many days I woke up with a face full of tears and many nights that I cried all night long until I fell asleep.

This went on for years. I was so miserable and felt like I was living in a world full of people but alone and sometimes invisible. The pain ran so deep I could not paint on a smile and pretend to be okay. I knew words of prayer, but I did not have the strength to pray for myself but thank God for my tribe. I remember hearing my husband praying for me every night, asking God to heal my broken heart and take the anger away. He would get in bed and hold me to bring some level of comfort to me.

I know that people were praying for me because, all of a sudden, I gained enough strength to start praying for myself again. Several years passed before this happened, though. After a while, I knew I had to ask God for forgiveness. I no longer felt like I didn't deserve to live or be happy. One day during prayer, God told me that there was nothing He needed to forgive me for, and it was time to forgive myself instead. God told me that none of what happened to my daughter was my fault and there was life after this for her and me. While this brought relief, the process of self-forgiveness was not easy, but it was an essential aid in my healing journey.

My steps to self-forgiveness included:

1. I continued to consult God for clarity, understanding, and peace within myself.
2. I was intentional about my communication with God.
3. I practiced honest self-reflection.
4. I took responsibility for the role I may have played.
5. I learned to accept what happened because I couldn't change anything.

These five steps were critical for my journey to self-forgiveness. I discovered multiple things I blamed myself for; however, these were not my baggage. I should've never taken ownership of any of these things. I had internalized many things in my life and accepted blame for them.

- My daughter was sexually assaulted as a child.
- I allowed people to treat me as less than others.
- I could not protect David from the cruelness of the world.
- I could not save David's life.

When God revealed these things to me, I was taken aback because I did not realize how much I blamed myself. Naturally, as a mother and a wife, my instinct was to protect my family, but in my eyes, I failed several times. What felt like a failure were opportunities for God to strengthen and build me back after life tore me down.

Studies have shown 62% of Americans struggle with self-forgiveness. Unresolved conflicts run deeper than you may realize, negatively affecting a person's overall health.

Forgiveness can positively affect someone's health by lowering their risk of heart attack, improving their cholesterol levels, and making them sleep better. Forgiveness can also help improve symptoms of anxiety, depression, and stress and reduce pain throughout the body. Self-forgiveness is such an active process that one must desire to forgive and be willing to commit to the process in its entirety, no matter if your focus is self-forgiveness or forgiving others.

I have learned the art of self-forgiveness and can now live outside the pain because my view is crystal clear as I look back from the other side of the struggle. I have gained so much knowledge, wisdom, and understanding. What happened to my daughter forced me to deal with myself and practice true self-forgiveness.

It is important to note that self-forgiveness is not a one-time event but an ongoing process. It requires continuous self-reflection, self-awareness, and a commitment to positively changing your life. Additionally, it may take time for you to fully let go of negative emotions and self-criticism. You may also need the support of others, such as a therapist or a support group.

Self-forgiveness is more than just putting the past behind you and moving on. It is about accepting what happened and showing compassion for yourself. Facing what you have done or what has happened is the first step towards self-forgiveness. There are four stages—I call them the four R's—of Self-Forgiveness.

1. Responsibility – Accept what happened and show yourself compassion. Grant yourself grace.
2. Remorse - Feeling remorse means you accept the role you played. Use it as a gateway to positive behavioral change.
3. Restoration - Make amends with yourself.
4. Renewal - List the lessons learned from the experience and grow from them.

Keep in mind that you will feel a variety of different emotions, and it is okay. Trust me, it's normal, and you must allow yourself to feel whatever arises at that moment. Do not try to suppress any of it. Understanding your emotions is an essential part of learning to forgive yourself.

Accepting responsibility for your actions is the hardest step but critical for self-forgiveness. This step forces you to look at yourself without excuses or rationalization, justifying your role and actions.

When you take responsibility and accept that your actions and decisions hurt others, you can better address the regret, guilt, and shame you will almost certainly feel. Again, this is completely normal because wrong is still wrong when you've done something intentionally or unintentionally. Knowing and understanding this will help lead to more positive feelings and behaviors.

Making amends is very important when it comes to self-forgiveness. If the situation involves offending or hurting others, you must apologize to them. Allow them to speak their peace and remember their feelings are, in fact, valid. Just know that whatever they say might not be pleasant or easy to hear. Sometimes the person you offended or hurt may never want to speak to you again, and that is okay because this step isn't about you. This is their right after what they experienced due to your words or actions. Most people can forgive others once they have received what they believe to be a genuine apology.

If you're the kind of person who can accept the role you played in someone else's trauma, you're most likely feeling anger, guilt, and even sadness about what happened. This is a good thing! The same rules apply to forgiving yourself. Apologize to yourself for the things you have done. Make peace with it all. Do things to make it up to yourself; simultaneously, you're showing yourself and anyone you hurt that you're a different person through your words and actions.

Rectifying your mistakes is one way to move past guilt. Although this may seem like there is no great benefit to you, it hugely benefits the person you have offended or hurt; by eliminating the attitude, words, and behaviors that caused the problem in the first place. You are taking important steps toward a better, more centered life for yourself. "I'm sorry" is a great place to start, but most people can't buy an apology because the person issuing it almost always repeats the behavior. Fixing your mistakes means you say you're sorry and show you mean it by not saying or doing ever again what caused the trouble in the first place.

By recognizing your mistakes and altering what you say and do, you eliminate the need to think you could have done more. Everyone has made a mistake or done something they wished they could take back, but not everyone will own up to it. Not everyone is willing to deal with themselves. Feeling sorry or regretful is normal. You must be careful not to fall into self-hatred like a trap or wallow in self-pity with overwhelming feelings of unworthiness and lack of motivation the way I did.

Self-forgiveness requires finding ways to sift through the mess of it all and pulling out the lessons so that you continue to grow from your experiences. On the journey to self-forgiveness, you must make daily active efforts to do better than you did before. You will have opportunities to prove to yourself that you have learned and grown from your mistakes.

Your emotional and psychological well-being cannot be fully realized without you forgiving yourself. You must acknowledge and accept your mistakes, express remorse, and make amends. You have to let go of negative emotions and self-criticism. By embracing the principles of self-forgiveness, you can move forward and grow from your experiences to cultivate greater self-awareness, compassion, and well-being.

Please know this advice is based solely on my journey toward self-forgiveness and healing. It was not easy, but it has been more rewarding than one could ever imagine. I stopped feeling like I should have been able to predict the future. Gone are the days when I felt unworthy of happiness and living a healthy and meaningful life. My mental health, physical health, and spiritual health have been restored. My marriage is healthy, and my children and grandchildren are well. My business is flourishing like never before.

None of this would have happened had I continued harboring unforgiveness in my heart towards myself, had I continued having the pity party, and had I not allowed God to come into my heart. If I am honest with myself, I don't think I would be alive today, but to God be the glory! He has given me life, new meaning, and purpose. God allowed me to extend grace to myself and walk in total forgiveness. This is the most liberating gift I could have ever received.

# Dedication

This chapter is dedicated to mothers that may have fallen short and made mistakes along the way, that posed a negative and painful ripple effect to your child/children, loved ones and most importantly yourself. Life doesn't come with instructions but fortunately for us, God grants grace, mercy and extends full forgiveness. I understand that you may not know where to start and it will not be easy but it's the best gift you can ever give yourself.

Shaquandra, thank you for loving me, granting me grace and giving me the opportunity to grow as a mother and to create beautiful memories together as mother and daughter.

Repeat this out loud:

God, I have been trying to forgive myself, but I still carry shame. Today I receive that gift of forgiveness you hold out to me. Thank you for doing a healing work inside of me that I cannot do on my own. Thank you for a new day, a new chapter and a new beginning. Thank you for allowing me the opportunity to understand that Self-forgiveness is the key that unlocks the chains to my past mistakes; liberating my spirit to embrace a magical future of growth and self-love.

# REFLECTIONS

# REFLECTIONS

# Celeste Dowdell

## Be Your Own Great Love

# Celeste Dowdell

## Be Your Own
## Great Love

*"He that getteth wisdom loveth his own soul: he that keepeth understanding shall find good"*

*Proverbs 19:8, KJV*

I looked for love and acceptance for most of my life to feel like I mattered.

When you don't feel like you're receiving love from the one place it should automatically be given, it does something to you on the inside. As a child, I didn't feel loved; I felt out of place or tolerated, and the one person who should have loved me the most didn't even like me. It wasn't a good feeling, so I decided if they didn't care about me, why should I care about anyone? I developed an attitude and kept most people at a distance.

For as long as I can remember, my family called me mean and hateful. When I was 17, I didn't see any point in living at home any longer; there wasn't anything uplifting or encouraging for me in that space. I had to figure it out independently, even though I had no plan other than finding a job and somewhere to live. I was close to graduating from high school and determined to make it on my own.

I started doing things I normally would not have done, acting out of character, hurting those I loved, and breaking bonds that meant a lot to me. I was depressed and didn't feel worthy of happiness. I didn't know my next move, but I was too proud to ask for help.

I bounced from job to job and stayed with friends until I started working at Home Depot and moved into my place. I thought things were looking up. I also started dating this guy I had known for a while. We had some good times, and about a year later, when I was 20, our little boy was born. I had a fairy tale in my mind about how I would finally have all the love I wanted. Our relationship was good until it wasn't, but I did all I could to make it work. I thought I was in love, but my son's father was yet another person who let me down. I was hurt, and my pain turned to anger, making me bitter. I was already defensive with my feelings, and our breakup made me want to put my wall back up and not let anyone else get close. A part of me figured I was still young, so maybe it wasn't meant to be right now.

I decided to stay guarded, take some time, and think about what I wanted and was looking for. I wanted that love-at-first-sight feeling, the butterflies-in-your-stomach kind of attraction, but I wasn't convinced those were real or just in the movies. I thought I'd have fun and live life with my son. I wanted to give him everything I didn't have. He would never wonder if I loved him. He would know I always had his back.

I kept that wall up for many years. I had to protect my heart and feelings, and I felt that if I was mean and standoffish, no one could get close enough to hurt me. I lived like this for so long; it was like a reflex. I was mean, but my hurt was so deep that I felt it was the only way to survive.

For years, people said I looked mean and unapproachable or that I was stuck up, and all of it was so far from the truth. I'm the most sensitive and caring person, but only those close to me were aware. I was doing things my way, and you either liked me or you didn't.

A few years later, I was hanging out with one of my sisters, and we decided to go out but away from home. We needed new scenery and to meet new people. So, we went to a club where we had drinks, danced, and sang loudly to every song. I'm not a dancer, but it was a great time. Suddenly, there he was, this young Dominican Papi dressed in Polo™ from head to toe and blinged out, giving me butterflies. My heart smiled again, and I had to know him. I walked to the bar near where he was standing to try and make eye contact, but I didn't need to try. I was already on his radar. His name was DP, we talked a little bit, and I thought he had a good vibe, so we exchanged numbers. Over the next two years, the chemistry between us was crazy. We spent a lot of time together and always had great conversations. I was infatuated, and there was nothing he wouldn't do for me except turn off that damn phone.

His phone kept ringing, and I found out DP was the plug! I liked things before I knew all of that. I am too nosey, lol. The chemistry never changed, but the vibe did. When I found out I was pregnant, I didn't think twice about it; I was happy. Unfortunately, my body had different plans, and I lost the baby. I was heartbroken and even more so because the dynamic between us was changing. I still don't know why. We never had a conversation about what was happening in our relationship, and any conversations we had became less frequent.

I remember being so angry that I opened my heart to someone for nothing. And even though the pregnancy wasn't planned, I looked forward to having another child. That feeling wasn't going away, so I thought I could have another baby with my son's father. Who knows? Maybe we could give things another shot. We had a second son, but the relationship didn't work out, and I was okay with that. There was a reason we weren't together, and he continued to be present in our boys' lives.

I felt good about being single. I spent time with my close friends and my kids. I was done opening my heart just to get hurt. I didn't want to be bothered because guys were all the same. I was mean to any guy who said "Hi," or asked how I was doing. I didn't care because no one was going to get the best of me again. The saying is true about hurt people, hurt people.

At the time, I worked for Cigna Healthcare and spent my free time with my boys. We went to the park, hung out at Chuck E. Cheese, and attended friends' and family's birthday parties. I had a good life, but I also never had much free time of my own. I decided to do something just for me: go on vacation and live my best life. I booked a group cruise as an early birthday gift to myself. A girlfriend and I flew to Jacksonville, FL, to meet my brother. I was excited to board the boat at the port, but he said we had to wait for his friend who was on a different flight.

"Well, he's about to get left. Who is this friend?"

"We're waiting for Trece."

I remembered him from school and thought he was cool, but when I saw him walking toward us, I swear it was like in the movies when the person started walking slowly. I ran to the bathroom to change my shirt to look nicer. I thought the next five days would be interesting, to say the least. I was not looking for anything serious and was determined to be single, but that's not how it worked out.

As always, it was great in the beginning. Four years later, we had a child and got along well, but it wasn't always fun and games, especially when he pointed out my bad attitude and how I was so mean to people. He said I always made this face and looked mad, but half the time, I didn't even know I was doing it. Some days, I was in a good mood, so I couldn't have been making "the face." Hearing him say these things repeatedly was very annoying. And you would think I might have stopped to think if what he said was true, but I just got more mad.

What made me pause was noticing my kids had mean faces, which annoyed me. Maybe what Trece said was true. I also couldn't ignore comments from other people about my children being as mean as I was and how they all had my attitude. These were not traits I wanted them to have, and I didn't want them to hear the same things I'd heard all my life. I never wanted them to be perceived as angry, especially because I was so careful to show them happiness and for them to know they were loved.
I didn't like this perception of me any more, and I realized my attitude was most likely the reason my circle of friends had gotten so small. My mean expression and funky vibe was "the joke," but I knew it was how people felt. People didn't like me. I needed to figure out why but didn't know where to start.

Watching 'Why Did I get Married?' helped.

In the movie, Janet Jackson's character explained how wives should make lists of the good and bad about their husbands. If the bad outweighed the good, they should let go of their marriage, but if the good outweighed the bad, they needed to work to repair their relationships. I decided to make this list about myself, and I just knew I was going to look great on paper. But as I went over my list, I wasn't looking that great. I realized I was not happy with my life or with myself. I didn't like me. I spent so many years keeping up a wall. How could anyone else like me? The defense mechanism I thought protected me all those years was the problem. I was tired of being angry and reacting with anger. I was in such a lonely space, even when surrounded by people I loved and cared about.

I knew I couldn't continue living this way and needed to figure out how to change, but I wasn't sure where to start. I had many restless nights and cried a lot of tears. I should have gotten therapy, but there was such a negative stereotype surrounding it. I also thought a stranger who didn't know me, what I was going through I was going through, hadn't seen my life or didn't know my circle, couldn't help me, but it was what I needed. Most of us need therapy, and I now know it's okay to seek help if you need it. I wish I knew then what I know now.

I started with a list of what I did and didn't like about my life. I knew I needed to check my attitude at the door. I needed to own things I wasn't proud of, including apologizing to a cousin who's trust I had broken when we were younger. She accepted my apology but wasn't open to having a relationship with me. It was one of the hardest things for me. Once I had done that, I had to decide what I wanted out of life beyond being happy and loved.

I had already found love a few times and been let down. I wanted to live life in a different way. I wanted to feel fulfilled, do something that mattered, and be known for something other than the mean girl. I needed to discover a new direction to become the woman I had always pictured myself as. Others had done it, so why couldn't I? I asked myself what would make me happy and how I could feel accomplished. I worried that it was too late.

I understood for too long; I accepted and even invited negativity into my life. I had to stop giving others power over my emotions. I started removing myself from situations instead of fighting for the situation to change. I started smiling more, even when life wasn't going my way. I learned the importance of changing my mindset so everything else could fall into place. I started thinking about all the things I never got the chance to do when

I was younger and things I had put off taking care of someone else's needs.

I started an online jewelry business, NuAttitude, by Celeste. I stepped outside my comfort zone, meeting and talking with new people. I never thought I was a people person, but I loved it. Covid hit, and my business took a backseat; things were slow, and I was in a funk. I felt lonely again and as if I had no purpose. I needed another outlet to give me purpose and a reason to leave the house. I wanted to do something meaningful and make a difference for someone else..

One of my cousins was a member of a non-collegiate sorority, and I loved their commitment to service, so I started looking for one in my area. I thought I could still have the sisterhood I would have had if I'd gone to college. I liked the service aspect of sororities and wanted to help others. I found two organizations, and the one I thought would be the best fit was The Philo Affiliate of Sigma Gamma Rho Sorority, Inc. after learning more about them. This would give me something to do that had meaning and the sorority feeling I always wanted. And now, I am one of the founding members of the Theta Alpha Sigma Philo Affiliate, the first chapter in Connecticut. I love my sisters and that we represent women's empowerment and community service. It's great when we do things in the community to make a difference for others.

I also wanted to expand my entrepreneurial experience by learning new skills. What better first step could I take than returning to school to get my degree? I'd always planned to earn my Bachelor's degree. Although I knew I could I could succeed without it, I also knew a college education would open doors I wanted to walk through.

I chose to stop waiting for the "right time" in order to do things. My happiness is no longer negotiable or something I will push to the side. I know it can and will happen with or without others. This journey for me isn't over. I still have work to do on myself and continue working toward being a better person.

I would tell anyone who might feel the way I felt not to let childhood traumas or emotions consume you. Talk about it, cry about it, and just let it out somehow because it will turn you into someone you won't recognize or like later.

Seek therapy because there is no shame in getting professional help. Try to be for others the person you want someone to be for you. You never know what someone might be going through. Say "Hi," to others or even give a smile. The little things could make someone's day. Be slow to anger, but don't let anyone play in your face. And don't give up on love. Yes, relationships are challenging, and you have to do your part. Who knows? It could be worth it.

They say you only get three great loves in life, but who knows? Maybe you need four or five. Don't wait for someone else to make you happy or to validate you. Make yourself laugh, buy yourself flowers. Be your own great love.

Book the trips. Laugh at your own jokes, even when they aren't funny. Take yourself out to eat. Make yourself a priority.
This is my season for self-love, and it's time for me to shine.

# Dedication

To my sons: RaQuan, Jaedon and Patrece Jr.

You are my main reason for change. Watching you grow from infancy to young men, made me take a deeper look into myself. Knowing that children model what they see, I wanted to make sure that I was doing my part to support how you show up in the world. Loving, supporting and taking care of you has always been a priority for me.

Life isn't always easy and you may hit some bumps along the way. However, I believe it's important to put out in the world what you would like to receive in return and to always put yourself first.

That's why it was so important for me to change what I felt like was no longer working for me and what I didn't like seeing. I encourage you to do the same. Always be the best version of yourself for yourself first and then for others.

Change takes time so thank you for your unconditional love, time and patience as I work through Becoming a better me: woman and mother!

# REFLECTIONS

_____

_____

_____

_____

_____

_____

_____

_____

_____

_____

_____

_____

_____

_____

_____

_____

_____

_____

_____

# REFLECTIONS

_____

_____

_____

_____

_____

_____

_____

_____

_____

_____

_____

_____

_____

_____

_____

_____

_____

_____

_____

_____

# Jacquelyn Santiago Nazario

## A Worthy and Hopeful Heart

# Jacquelyn Santiago Nazario

## A Worthy and Hopeful Heart

*"We often block our own blessings because we don't feel inherently good enough or smart enough or pretty enough or worthy enough.. you're worthy because you are born and because you are here. You're being here, your being alive makes worthiness your birthright. You alone are enough" -Oprah Winfrey*

I hid in the corner of the library at my new private school. I gripped The Color Purple tight. My eyes jumped around the pages. I could not put the book down. Celie knew my secret. Her father sexually abused her just as a man my parents trusted had done to me.

This person was supposed to be my caretaker while my parents were working. Instead, he took his sexual gratification with my body. I was six. I could not tell a soul. I would be responsible for the destruction of our family.

I felt ashamed, guilty, unworthy of the love and did not know how a good girl like me could cause so much trouble. My rapist manipulated my mind and emotions by threatening me with the only thing he could: the love of my family. I remember he sat on the edge of the bed after violating me on what seemed like a daily practice after my parents left for work. He caressed my hair and handed me a coloring book, crayons, and a Strawberry Shortcake doll. Her hair was yarn, and she smelled like fresh strawberries. He made sure I knew that if I ever told anyone about him forcing me to have sex with him, my parents would believe his denials. He would tell them that I was confused and ungrateful, that all he ever did was care for me with pure intentions. When he gave me the gifts, I did wonder if I truly was an ungrateful or evil person, and I knew my parents would believe him. I could hear my father telling me, "Children are seen and not heard." As a female child, especially, I knew my voice did not matter.

Even as a child, I understood the messages all around me. Some of the lessons came through direct observations about how to act as a faithful wife. Responsibilities included cooking, cleaning, and serving a husband and children. My older sister and I followed everything our mother did while my two younger brothers were responsible for nothing and encouraged to be dominant. According to tradition and the Bible, women were supposed to submit to their husbands in every way. In fact, it was strictly prohibited for women to voice an opinion contrary to any "facts" spoken by the head of the household. Some of the most common Puerto Rican refrains talked about how women looked prettier with closed mouths. When my mother disagreed with my father, he drove that lesson home by cursing her, pinning her to the wall, and threatening her life. I recall countless stories of women who cast their dreams aside because their roles were isolated to motherhood and common-law wife. I discovered that a broken heart could still keep a woman alive to fulfill her duties. I also knew that speaking to God or drowning my tears in the shower were the only safe places to voice my thoughts or display the pain in my heart.

In fifth grade, I received a scholarship to an elite private school in North Andover, Massachusetts. Pike School was 15 minutes away from Lawrence, my poor mill city. However, it was a world away from the poverty, pain, and Puerto Rican traditions that surrounded me at home. My mother forced me to attend despite the fact I was unhappy that no one looked or spoke like me. She immediately began the transfer when she discovered I won a scholarship to attend the private school. She dismissed my pleas to stay at my old neighborhood school with my friends and the teachers I loved. Dad was in sync with my mother's decision because they knew this school could be a pathway out of poverty for my family. She told me that one day I would understand the sacrifice.

I longed to see other brown-skinned classmates who understood when I had to use a Spanish word for the English one I did not know. My new classmates were cruel, ridiculed my Spanish accent, poked fun at my thrift store clothing, and threw food in my hair. My coarse hair fascinated the kids who threw things because of how everything caught in it. I heard them refer to me as the Black girl, and for the first time, I wondered why my skin was so much darker than that of my blue-eyed classmates.

My search for answers about who I was led me to that library where I found The Color Purple and books about slavery. I lost myself in those pages as I marveled at the use of language and the raw emotions displayed through the author's writing. I couldn't believe someone allowed the use of swear words and that the authors freely described their pain for others to feel. I cried as I found an escape from both of my worlds and I felt the words in the depth of my soul where I had never been before. Reading about what happened to me gave me the words, but I didn't use them until many decades in the future.

It seems that the more answers I found, the more questions I had. I loved this journey of exploration and learning because I felt a comforting personal power. This quiet power allowed me to learn myself and discover a future filled with possibility. The physical separation from the sources of my pain allowed me to begin healing in a way I had never imagined. At home, I made myself useful, hid my secret, and kept the love of my family. Despite everything, I wanted them to be proud of me.

No one ever noticed all my moments of solitude, the desire to protect my siblings, that I distrusted almost everyone, or my extreme need to control everything. My parents assumed that these traits were a part of my emerging personality.

My effort and curiosity led to another scholarship to a private high school 40 minutes away. Pingree School offered a quality education, after-school sports, and small classroom settings with affluent white classmates. Pingree was an elevated level of wealth; young people drove their brand-new Mercedes and BMWs to school. I had no choice but to ride the bus for an hour to school every day. Those bus rides were a frantic sprint to complete homework assignments or try to participate in conversations with classmates about liberties and activities their parents provided them. I could never relate to any freedom as I was bound to caring for siblings, cooking, and cleaning to help my mother. We also had lots of family visiting, eating, and storytelling, but nothing anyone on that bus could identify with. I caught the bus at a parking lot and was the first one picked up on the bus every morning, so that gave me radio control. I turned the dial to Hot 94.5 and then sat in the back seat listening to hip-hop and R&B music.

The white kids would pick fights about the music on the radio and say my music was garbage and made no sense. I never fought back; I told myself they did not know real music. Eventually, I started carrying a Walkman and headphones on the bus to clear the noise. Sometimes, I listened to their music and appreciated Nirvana and other rock-and-roll music I had never listened to before. I did everything I could to stay out of the way, but this one boy, Mike, still found ways to poke under my skin to find my vulnerabilities.

He always had unkind words and was the bus megaphone. I heard him talk about how creepy looking my dad was. Something snapped inside me, and I beat him in the head and upper body with my Walkman. The music stopped, and the cover buckled, but I could not hear everyone screaming for me to stop. I did not halt until the door fell off the Walkman and the headphone's wires split to the port. Mike's ridicule swept through my body and up my spine like a 140-degree infrared heatwave. It stopped at my chest like a fireball that sparked an explosion that could only be relieved by hitting him so he could feel even a little of my pain. Of course, beating Mike with my Walkman did not stop the pain. I felt crazed because I knew Mike's comments were mostly true, which is true of so much shame. My family had some serious dysfunction, and now others knew it, too. My dad had exposed us through his actions in front of my classmates.

A few weeks earlier, I was taking the activities bus home, and it dropped me off at the bus stop where other students were also picked up by their parents. My dad was waiting for me in an old car with his drinking buddies. It was only 6 p.m., and they were already in no condition to drive. My dad and his friends stared at the bus for over five minutes, willing me down the steps and out the door. Dad could not get out of the car to get me because he couldn't walk. Mike said, "Who are those bums looking at us like that?" I turned to see my dad peering through the window. Without a word, I jumped off the bus and apologized to my dad, who was yelling at me for wasting his time. It was one of many frightening car rides home. I knew my family had generational curses around drugs and alcohol. It did not make living with the disease any easier, and I knew hiding it all from the world was better.

Friends could not visit me at home, I dared not share stories about home with my classmates, and my family would not come to school unless mandated. It was best for my family and me. I never truly felt safe or like I belonged anywhere despite finding those books in the library of my old school. The turmoil in my brain, body, and soul never seemed to rest. At home, I knew I had to carry the family secrets with my siblings; our dad's alcoholism and abuse, our parents' lack of education, and our poverty.

The heaviest burden was the one I carried alone. I cried to myself, thinking I was worthless and that I would never be enough. Who would want a damaged little girl like me? My mother explained that every woman's first responsibility was to learn to care for her home, husband, and children. Good women were pure, saved themselves for marriage, and looked to God for guidance during tough times. She said God always had a special place for obedient and pure women. I knew I had already failed to save myself for marriage. I hoped someone could love me one day since I started at age 10 to cook, clean, and care for my siblings.

The memories of being raped repeatedly tormented me daily, and I hid my appearance and voice as a result. I grew up faster than any child should have, which changed my personality. I craved love and acceptance, so I aimed to please, which meant overextending myself and apologizing when I was not at fault. I also had adult responsibilities, like caring for my younger brothers and my elderly grandparents, when I was still a child myself. Like most kids of my generation, I was taught to welcome everyone with a kiss. After my experience, I did not want to show love to many people, but I had to do it because of tradition and expectations.

At home, my family saw a smart girl with skills, someone they could depend on. The person I identified with was not the one my classmates saw when I was at school. They saw a poor, dysfunctional, Black girl who could not keep up with the academic rigor. I found the real me somewhere in the middle of those versions. I juggled shame, rejection, and anger; simultaneously, I found opportunities to learn more about my heritage, passions, and myself. I waited out the bad moments as best I could and cast aside negative self-talk just long enough to listen to the lessons in school. I loved learning and was curious but struggled to focus and meet my fullest potential.

I never truly caught up from my poor early childhood education, and the traumas I experienced made me cautious around men, worried about who would exploit me, and constantly scanning for anyone who might hurt me. I told myself I would never voluntarily join a conflict, but I was prepared to kill it if it came looking for me. Living in constant survival mode made it difficult for me to thrive. I know now that my mental health was impacted as well as my physical health. My body was constantly pumping cortisol (stress hormone) into my system, and it rewired my brain. Science shows that chronic stress and trauma restructure the brain to focus on survival rather than learning new information. Both inhibit our short-term memory and judgment skills.

I struggled as much in high school as in middle school. I learned about Manifest Destiny: how American Conquistadors took over lands to make the indigenous inhabitants "educated and civilized." While I identified with the indigenous people, I did not feel my opinion was valued, so I preferred to remain silent. "I look prettier with my mouth closed," I told myself.

Everything changed when I met Laura Eagle, a teacher who studied Spanish literature and history. She had visited many Spanish-speaking countries and noticed my withdrawal in class, so she gave me a special lunch invitation to read with her in Spanish. She explained the beauty of our culture and expressed gratitude for her lived experience in Puerto Rico. Mrs. Eagle gained my respect because she found beauty in my culture and me.

This kind, older white woman taught me to have pride in my roots. I confided in her about feeling isolated, rejected, and worthless. Her response was a firm hug. She told me, "You are a princess from a paradise full of strong people."

I started speaking more in class and sitting in front instead of hiding in the back. I started to feel a duty to educate people about the beauty of my language and traditions. I also started feeling responsible for guiding new students of color as they arrived. I taught them to make friends with the lunch staff so they could have more delicious, free food. I gave them what I didn't have when I arrived, ensuring they knew how to prepare for tests and class discussions and providing a rundown of the best teachers. A group of us started to meet to discuss our experiences at the school and plan school dances.

In my last year of high school, I decided to speak at a few school assemblies about my culture and the difficulty of transitioning to largely white, affluent schools. I cried during my presentations, surprising myself because I never allowed anyone to see my true self. The reality is that most of my fellow students could not understand or feel my struggle, but I no longer cared about that fact. I emerged stronger from the experience.

I felt like I could speak to anyone from any background. I found my voice amid a messy story and an ugly cry. I knew the pain in my school story could help others because there was power in my vulnerability. I felt as if sharing the story meant that I had some control. If I could be the author of my story, then no one could really hurt me.

If the veil of shame lifted off my face, I would be able to receive myself, accept myself, forgive myself, and love myself. Those were heavy thoughts, laden with centuries of ancestral baggage and childhood trauma. It took me five more years to develop the strength to understand and overcome most of it.

During my last year of high school, I made it clear that I was going to college and only applied to schools within the Boston area to appease my parents. They were hesitant about the distance but finally gave up the fight we had been having for over a year. I attended Trinity in Hartford, Connecticut, because they offered the most financial aid. My parents struggled because they valued education yet felt a woman should not be so far from her family, and eventually, they agreed with me.

My years in college were full of lessons about race, ethnicity, love, and gender. I embraced everything with a small group of close friends and enjoyed the liberty of living two hours away from home at school.

My family bonds and traditions kept me worried about everyone in my family but myself. I returned to Lawrence often, and when I was not at home, I worried about what difficult situation I couldn't resolve from a distance. My grades began to suffer, and one of my professors suggested I focus only on my education. He told me that if I always intervened on behalf of my family, they would never build their strength and ability to manage their dysfunctional behavior.

At the time, I cursed him for not understanding, but I changed my mind when I faced academic probation and the possibility of expulsion from school. I knew I had to make a major change in order to heal and excel. I became a good student, created healthy habits, and distanced myself from my family's disruptive behavior. The healing I felt in middle and high school started again when I learned to take walks by myself, speak to my best friend about my fear, and I fell in love with someone.

We became engaged, but as we planned our wedding and went to pre-marital counseling, I felt like a fraud because the man I was going to marry did not know the six-year-old me who had lost her innocence. Would he and his church still accept my damaged soul if he knew?

I confessed my story to him. Through his tears, he offered to help me continue healing. He said his little Jackie was strong, but I felt like a new person who needed to let that little hurt girl go.

I committed to counseling and came up with a plan to tell my family after my wedding so they could see I was victorious over my lifelong trauma. Destiny had different plans for me.

I was living a dream, as I was one of the few women in my family who would get to marry in a church with a white dress and her loved ones. The wedding rehearsal was wonderful, and I drove to my parent's house for a restful night's sleep before my beautiful, life-changing day. As I parked, my mom exclaimed, "I have a surprise for you!" I sensed family members walking toward me, but the only one I could see was the "friend" who raped me. I froze in place, and tears streamed down my face. I could barely talk. Everyone assumed that the happiness overwhelmed me as I ran upstairs crying.

My mom followed me, thinking I was upset that she invited them. The only thing I could do was to ask her to take a drive with me. I told her everything between sobs. She remained silent as if to choke back her tears. My mom said she always feared the man had uncontrollable urges and hoped I could forgive him. I waited 17 years to reveal the pain and imagined a long talk, but I realized I was on the edge of a new life in that space. I knew I had to acknowledge my experience and continue taking steps to heal myself.

My mom lived a hard life, and she taught me to be a warrior and overcome anything. No matter the struggle, she would say, "Do not drown in a glass of water." There was never a challenge too great. She was strong, and my revelation did not break her. She hugged me when we got out of the car, and we did not speak about it again. It took me another couple of decades to tell my father and siblings. They were amazed at my resilience and hurt that I didn't offer them the opportunity to protect me and show me love.

I felt different walking back inside the house. That man could not hurt me anymore. He could not destroy my family. I was not six years old anymore, and I had knowledge, self-love, a career, and a new life. The real issue was that I held onto the veil of shame and guilt and hurt myself as a result.

I felt sorry for him and his life circumstances. He had not found self-love, love, or success and struggled with mental health and generational curses.

I decided to forgive him. I also forgave myself for being a little girl who was threatened into not speaking a truth that could have saved others from the same fate.

I realized that my true personal power would never fully emerge until I forgave first. Months after beginning my healing journey, I transformed my pain into purpose. I became aware of the impact trauma had on my life, realized I was capable of helping myself, and utilized my experience to help others as a volunteer mentor of girls who had experienced similar trauma.

I taught them how to see the beauty in themselves and to reframe their negative thoughts and low self-esteem into empowerment.

I never harbored any resentment toward my parents.
I understood my parents could only teach me the things they had learned. I will always love them. The generational trauma each of my parents faced was almost impossible to overcome; however, they successfully raised their children.

I discovered that I could choose to become a victor and not a victim of my history. I was grateful for the opportunity to learn and grow.

I found the courage to speak and fight for what I believed in. Since high school, I've never missed an opportunity to do community service and help those stuck in the void of forgotten zip codes. My testimony confirmed that youths could flourish and thrive if provided with the resources, opportunities, and caring people to support them.

Today, I am the CEO of COMPASS Youth Collaborative, a Hartford non-profit organization that works with disconnected youth. My hope is that young people will find beauty and strength in their history, get the healing and support needed to build their personal power and grow into healthy and happy futures.

# Dedication

I am dedicating this chapter to my beloved parents. It is difficult to describe the incredible strength of my love for them. Life taught us all harsh lessons but we overcame the obstacles due to the power of the love we have for one another. My parents gave me everything they learned and possessed. Without their love, drive, and support, I would not be the person I am today. I owe them both my life and I promise to be the best person that I can be.

Love Always,
Your Grateful Daughter

# REFLECTIONS

_____

_____

_____

_____

_____

_____

_____

_____

_____

_____

_____

_____

_____

_____

_____

_____

_____

_____

_____

_____

_____

# REFLECTIONS

# Ann-Gela Holloway

## Speak Life and Believe in the Impossible!

# Ann-Gela Holloway

## Speak Life and Believe in the Impossible!

*"Death and life are in the power of the tongue: And they that love it shall eat the fruit thereof"*
*Proverbs 18:21 KJV*

How did I become Her?

Well, I spoke her into existence! I hear you saying, "It can't be that easy?" You are right, and it has not been that easy. So, let me take you on a journey—my journey.

When I was nine, my eldest brother graduated from high school. His best friend at the time graduated first in their class. As a valedictorian, she earned a full, four-year academic scholarship to Yale University. Everyone was so proud of her and happy for her. She was indeed brilliant and a super kind person. While I was very happy for her, I also had my future in my sights. I told myself I wanted a full, four-year scholarship when I went to college. How did that statement sound to you? You are correct if you think that statement sounded bold and audacious!

It was so bold and audacious that I never even spoke it out loud. And, to be honest, I probably only said it once. I thought about it when we were at the awards ceremony for my brother and his friend. The thought then left me soon after.

It was also a bold and daring statement since, despite my intelligence, I had the self-assurance of a turtle taking part in a

NASCAR race. I lacked confidence in myself. I always told myself that I was "inner city" smart. I said that because I felt the public school system did not challenge us. So, in my mind, my good grades would not measure up against the brilliant and rich kids in the world. Speaking of rich, that is another reason why that statement was so audacious. I already knew at nine years old that we were poor. I knew that college would have to be on someone else's dime, or else it was not going to happen. In that brief moment, I was bold and audacious enough to ask for what I wanted and needed. What in the world was I thinking?

Fast forward to nine years later into my high school graduation, Would you like to guess what happened? Well, if you guessed that I graduated as valedictorian of my class, you are correct! I graduated first in my class and was awarded a full, four-year scholarship to a University! No, it wasn't Yale University. I went to a better school–Virginia Union University. VUU is an HBCU in Richmond, Virginia. The location of that school was also important, and I'll get to the significance of that later in my story.

I was 18 years old at the time, and I had a full scholarship to go to college. The idea was to major in computer engineering, launch my dot-com, and live happily off the income of my business. Wow, that was a wonderful plan. However, a wonderful plan doesn't make for a good story, does it?

In August of 1995, my family drove onto the beautiful campus of VUU, and I was blown away! Please understand that this was my first time seeing the campus in person. I mentioned that my family was poor, so there was no opportunity to visit the school beforehand. It was a walk of faith that brought me that far. I stayed in the honors dorm along with other full scholarship recipients. I enjoyed being a part of such Black excellence. I experienced everything for the first time, from Black Greek life to Friday night football games with marching bands. I thanked God for the opportunity to start a new life in a new state, with a new state of mind.

However, when the semester finished in May of 1996, my mom drove to Virginia to pick me up. I said goodbye to all of my friends. It was 'goodbye, and not 'see you later, because I was leaving campus six months pregnant. In addition to being pregnant, I had also not fulfilled my obligation to keep my GPA above 3.5. My less-than-satisfactory grades were due to my pregnancy too. Morning sickness, depression, and long afternoon naps had me missing classes and assignments. It was undoubtedly a very tough time in my life. Unfortunately, my tough times was just beginning.

I am going to continue with my story, just know that during this challenging time in my life, my faith was non-existent. My hope had dried up like a puddle after a storm. I had no desire to 'speak life. In fact, during that time, I spoke very negatively about myself and my circumstances. I mean, it was my fault that I was pregnant. I could only hold myself accountable for allowing my grades to slide. I even wondered why I had ever received a full scholarship in the first place. I was stupid and irresponsible. I had fallen into a deep depression and felt stuck in my circumstances. I had forgotten how to dream big.

In the fall of 1997, I was working in fast food. My salary was four dollars and seventy-seven cents an hour. I worked part-time, so my paychecks were barely two hundred dollars. I also collected welfare. My welfare check was an additional four hundred and forty-three dollars monthly. I gave my mother four hundred dollars for rent each month. I also received eighty-three dollars worth of food stamps. In those days, there was an eighteen-month cap on welfare benefits. At the end of my eighteen months, I had an appointment with a welfare-to-work counselor. During my appointment, the counselor tried to match me with a suitable training program that would grant me a certificate within six to eight weeks. I will never forget our conversation as she looked through the binder of programs to find one that matched my skills and desired job goal. She eventually closed the book.

"These programs aren't for you. You, you need to be in college."

Boom! There it was! Her words kindled a flame within me that I had no idea existed. Getting pregnant, dropping out of college, and returning home to work in fast food was a huge cloud of shame in my life. NO ONE told me that everything was going to be okay. NO ONE hugged me and told me that they were proud of me. I got hit with a fiery dart after a fiery dart. Many of those darts I threw at myself.

But, at that moment, I felt different. I felt seen, I felt loved, and I felt encouraged. When I left my appointment, I decided to apply to college again for the spring semester. While waiting for my bus downtown, I called my mother from a payphone.

"Mom, I am going to SCSU (Southern Connecticut State University) next semester!"

"Huh? How did that happen? Did you apply? Were you accepted?"

"Nope! I haven't applied yet or anything. I know that I'm going", and I DID!

I enrolled in classes at Southern CT State University in January 1998. I studied computer science and graduated in 2002. The words of the counselor in that office gave me back my ability to speak. And I spoke a few things over my life, like college, a car, and a wonderful new relationship. At that time, I also joined the church and began to work in ministry.

Of course, with the cycle of life, I found myself in a bad place again. And, as much as I could try to blame someone else, my choices resulted in me losing nearly everything.

The years between 1998 and 2004 were pretty good. I experienced some firsts. I experienced some, I-will-not-do-that again! I grew in my faith; I was raising my son, survived Y2K, and embarked on a lifestyle change where I lost fifty pounds!

In 2000 I began to work at my first full-time job. Then, in 2003 I took a second part-time job and had two incomes. It was a great time. I bought a car that I did not have to share–in the past, my sister and I shared a car. I had money to do fun and exciting things with my son. I met some very good people at both jobs, some that I am still in contact with today. And then, I met this guy.

Before discussing my relationship with this guy, let me give you more background about myself. With all of the beautiful achievements that I listed, there always felt to be one thing missing. That thing was love and marriage. If I can be honest, those were two separate things. I wanted marriage, and as long as that marriage looked good, it meant that I was not alone. So, love was not the priority. Earlier in this chapter, I wrote that I had the confidence of a turtle competing in a NASCAR race, which means I had zero confidence! And my self-esteem was not only low but also negative, non-existent if you will. I had convinced myself that life was not worth living if I did not have a man. Non-existent self-esteem also told me that I was single because I was ugly. So, it is easy to see why I just wanted anyone who could validate my existence on Earth and to make my life worth living.

Now that I've given you some background information, allow me to tell you about my relationship with this man. He played the villain in my story for many years. He was the one who lied and hurt me. The truth, however, is that I lied to and hurt myself. I remembered that my life went in the direction of my most powerful thoughts. I was simply the victim of my insecurities. Now, without making him the villain, let me tell the story. I met this guy—let me give him a name—Buck. I met Buck at a Burger King parking lot on my lunch break. I was getting in my car, and he stopped to talk to me. It was pouring rain that day. That should have been flag number one. Any woman who knows her worth would not stand in the rain to talk to a random guy. However, we already established that I did not know my worth. Buck had five children and was a few months home from prison. He worked at a factory in town that was known for hiring felons. We dated for a few months, and we talked about marriage. I gave him money a few times. The first time he told me that he went to the ATM to get his rent money. The ATM made a noise but did not spit out the bills. He was desperate. So, I gave him the money until the bank could clear up the malfunction. They never cleared it up because he never paid me back. At another time, I gave him a more significant amount, around twelve hundred dollars. This money was part of my security deposit for our apartment, so it wasn't only for him. Recall that we discussed getting married. In actuality, I believed we were engaged.

One night in July of 2004, I was supposed to meet Buck at his place to spend the night. He got off work at eleven o'clock, but it was almost midnight, and he was not home yet. We had cell phones back then, so I called him a few times with no answer. I took the liberty to drive by his ex-wife's house. When I pulled up, his car was outside. She answered the door, laughed, and let him know that I was outside. He came to the door and yelled at me. I yelled and cried back. His ex-wife assured me that she did not want any drama. Then, Buck headed to his car to leave. I got in my car too, but I saw him turn off his engine and exit his car. He was going back into her house. I snapped! I revved the engine and tried to run him over. He jumped to avoid being hit and referred to me as a crazy lady.

I left, but I did not go home. I drove around and cried. And for some reason, I drove by Buck's place again. This time his car was outside, as well as his ex-wife's car. I snapped for a second time that night. I called him, threw rocks at his window, and rang the doorbell to his place. For reference, his place was a rooming house. I was standing outside at one in the morning, ringing the doorbell repeatedly. I could have been arrested. I could have been shot for waking up his roommates, who had nothing to do with my drama. Needless to say, he did not come outside to talk to me. I snapped a third time.

Earlier in my story, I mentioned that I was working my first full-time job. That job was at AAA motor club. My job was to dispatch tow trucks. I worked there for four years and had a rapport with my co-workers and most tow truck drivers. That night I used my influence to request a tow truck. I told them that my boyfriend lost the keys to his car, and we needed to tow his car to my house. The truth was, I had them tow away his ex-wife's car. I did this because I wanted her to wake up the next morning to find her car gone. Yes, I already acknowledged that I was a crazy lady and clearly not too crazy. Because after the car was towed away, I went to my job. I eventually told my co-workers what I had done. I requested that the car be towed back to the pick-up address.

My co-workers flipped out on me. What I did was a crime. And they were unknown accessories to that crime. The police were called, but thankfully, they did not file charges. More than any sort of stealing, the crime was domestic in nature. Her car was intact, in place, and I was able to go home that night. Although there were repercussions from that evening, I was dismissed due to my actions. My manager and I had a meeting, and they required some time to classify what I did. I had committed a new violation that did not fit under any specific action in our employee handbook. I guess that I am a bit of a history-maker!

I can laugh now, but getting fired was not funny. The night I was fired, I bought a bottle of Tylenol PM and I drove to the hospital emergency room. The intention was to take the pills and then go inside to let them know what I did if they were able to save me in time; great. If not, great too. Because I had nothing to live for except my son, and I had let him down already. In spite of the heaviness that I felt, I decided not to take the pills. By that time, it was close to five in the morning, and the gym was open. So, I chose to go there and work out before I went home.

I was living paycheck to paycheck like the majority of folks. And when the paychecks stopped, I was broke. I ended up returning the unopened bottle of Tylenol PM to the store. I needed that $4.99! While I was broke, I was also heartbroken. The man that I snapped for wanted nothing to do with me. He also swore that we were not engaged. It was his word against mine then because there was no ring. I accepted not having a ring because I was okay without one. As I've stated before, I just wanted a man. I never asked for a healthy relationship. At this time, I had no credibility. I had demonstrated that I could not be trusted. So, who would believe me over him?

From July until November 2004, I was without a job. I lived with my mother at the time. Although I did not have to worry about being evicted, living off her was hard for my son and me. I applied for unemployment, but my case was denied. I will also never forget that unemployment hearing. We all knew the reason for my being fired. But, I was shocked when the company representative had documentation of other light things I had never been written up for. They already had a strong enough case; it hurt that they were willing to further drag my name through the mud. Again, I was not a victim. I caused all of this. But I will not lie and say that it did not hurt.

One night in October, I prayed after my car had been repossessed. I never stopped going to church or believing in God. In fact, during my time of being unemployed, I read the Bible a lot. I can still quote scriptures today that I meditated on during that time. This night while in prayer, I felt in my spirit that God was asking me to write down everything wrong with my life. To write down everything that I wanted God to do. It was a long list. Some of the items on the list were:

· Bank account overdrawn

· $10 in my pocket

· Car repossessed

· Living with my mom

· Heartbroken

· Unemployed

I wrote these things down, and I believed God! The next day–

the very next day, I received an invitation to apply for a job. Back then, that was the procedure for State jobs. You took an exam for different job classes. And if you passed the exam, your name was put on a list for State agencies to choose from whenever they had an opening. I applied for the job, had an interview, and was hired! My old salary at my previous job was around $20,000 a year. This new job started at $30,000. Within two years, I was making $45,000, which was more than double my salary. Since then, I am still employed by the State Government, I have been promoted six times. I currently make more than six figures, and I am rising. Let me list a few more achievements:

· Homeowner

· Got Married

· Put my oldest son through college

· Starred in a stage play

· The commencement speaker at my Alma Mater's graduation.

· Published a book

· Started a podcast

· Started a business

· I got a passport and traveled internationally

· Owned several cars– paid off two of them

· Ordained as a Minister

· Life Coach

I moved from broke and broken to becoming HER! I changed my thoughts. Those thoughts changed my words. The words changed my actions. My actions brought success. And whenever I find myself in a difficult place, I wash, rinse, and repeat. I've been in many difficult places since 2004. None as bad as that period because I changed. My life moved in the direction of my most powerful thoughts.

Allow me to leave you with a few points you can refer to. These are life lessons that I learned from experience.

1.  Walk with integrity. If anyone says anything negative about you, let it be a lie.

2.  Trust your Gut. It won't let you down. It has as much to lose as you do.

3.  You deserve to be treated well by others and by Yourself.

4.  Think before you speak. Think before you act. Not everything is reversible.

5.  It takes one moment to change your life. Run from foolish quests. Embrace wise opportunities.

6.  For every 'Yes that you give, there is a corresponding 'No. Be sure to live with the 'no before you say 'Yes.

# Dedication

I would like to dedicate my chapter to my late Sister Jennifer Holloway. Jenn was with me throughout my entire journey of becoming Me.

# REFLECTIONS

_____

_____

_____

_____

_____

_____

_____

_____

_____

_____

_____

_____

_____

_____

_____

_____

_____

_____

_____

# REFLECTIONS

# REFLECTIONS

# Shawn Goines-Rozetta

## Time for Change

# Shawn Goines-Rozetta

## Time for Change

*"Do not grieve, for the Joy of the Lord is your strength"*
*Nehemiah 8:10*

Although raised in the church and growing up in the North end of Hartford, I started hanging around older people at a young age, which showed me a different lifestyle. A lifestyle that included selling drugs and living a fast life. Because I didn't know anything different, I became attracted to this lifestyle, thinking and believing it was a "positive" thing to do. Everyone seemed to be living this way, and because everyone was doing it, I figured it was normal.

I was drawn to that life. I saw people getting beaten, shot at, murdered, using drugs, and selling drugs. You name it, and I've probably witnessed it. Then at the tender age of 15, I got pregnant and had my first daughter at 16. I was a teenage mother still trying to figure out life with a baby on my hip. My mom and sisters were very supportive in helping me raise my daughter. I was going to school, but I had no teenage life.

Fast forward to years later, I eventually graduated from high school but resorted to what I had witnessed around me growing up. I started selling drugs, drinking, partying, socializing with everyone, and being "that chic." "That chic" means living a fast life and having the freedom to go from one neighborhood to another without beefing with people. During the mid 80's in my time in the north end of the city, I carried myself with respect and integrity despite all of the drama that was going on around me. Geographical rivalries of the inner city, with streets and hoods fighting each other, I was still friends with everyone. Because of my relationship with everyone, I was sometimes the mediator between quarrels trying to keep the peace.

I thought I had it going on for me. I thought I was slicker than the capital letter S on Slick. I was nonchalant with unfiltered language. I was hanging with toxic people because, at the time, it was fun. I thought and felt I was "that chic" in this life. Being a teenage mom, I had to be responsible. My mother wasn't playing, though. I had to take my daughter to work with me sometimes, which helped me become more mature. I grew up fast and was labeled as fast.

As I grew older and started experiencing more of life, I started changing my mind about desiring and wanting to be "that chic." The chic was still drinking, partying, selling drugs, and living a fast life. However, life was catching up with me. I got pregnant again, married, and started hanging with certain people, and I felt like I was losing myself. I began to realize that I was not OK. I was so busy running around and caring for others that I lost myself. Who was checking on me? I was not taking care of myself to my fullest potential. I didn't get the rest I needed or eat properly because I always had someone else's needs on my mind. I was never calm or at peace because I always thought of the next move or another strategy. Even in my sleep, I was not at ease. For a while, things seemed as though they were connecting. I now had three children, a job, a husband, a home, a car, and money. I had what appeared to be all the things people longed to have, but something inside me didn't feel right.

I was feeling empty of myself. 'Shawn' was missing. The image that everyone else was looking for was starting to fade away.

I realized that being "that chic" was a mentality of "BEING STUCK." It was the mentality of having a certain character and style, maintaining a certain image, and being in "the life". The finances were there, but I should have made better decisions and investments with what I had. I went from place to place, barely resting and moving fast. All of a sudden, I took a step back and asked myself, "What are you doing?" "Where are you going?" With three kids later, I thought I was all that and a bag of chips. I was not focusing on the results. I was not focusing on my future. I realized there were certain things I no longer wanted for my life because I was living in the moment and not realizing that things could be gone at any minute. Then what? I failed to realize that my experiences and choices would shape all of my tomorrows. Stability was missing, and the assurance of a solid foundation. Yup, it was time for a change.

I wanted my children to see me differently. I stopped hanging out with certain people. I stopped hanging out at the clubs. I stopped selling drugs. I got another job to keep myself occupied. I wanted to go back to school and gain more education. I wanted to be different, and now wanting different eventually led to the decision to divorce because of the dysfunction and trauma experienced in the relationship.

My life was now turned upside down. I was disappointed and felt broken. I blamed myself and became more withdrawn from people. I stopped socializing. I got another job to keep myself occupied as I worked to change myself. All I was doing was going to work, church, and home. I started reading and studying the Bible more. However, I thought life was about work, work, and more work. And although this became my routine, and I was now occupied, it didn't replace the feelings of loneliness, disappointment, and brokenness. It wasn't easy. Even today, times can be challenging, but I try to stay focused on what I am supposed to be doing and my goals and dreams for my life. I've lived on both sides. While it was good and exciting back then, it was not fulfilling. Honestly, I once regretted my life.

Broken and crying, I had to start understanding myself, including joy, peace, happiness, sadness, fears, and standards. I felt that understanding those things would allow me to know more about myself to feel good about myself. I knew God called me for something better, but I didn't know how to get there. Don't get me wrong, I always believed, but I was not doing my best at honoring Him. Once I started allowing God to help me figure out who I am supposed to be and why I am here on Earth, I felt I was being transformed and not conformed. There were many things that I would have to change; friends, the places I would go, the things that I would do, my thinking, my walking, my talking. Before, I thought I was in control by doing what I wanted and knew what was best for me. I had to realize someone else was in control. I increasingly depended on God with all my heart, mind, and soul. He was able to guide me, lead me, redirect me, and assure me that I was not walking alone.

### Then and Now

As a natural-born caretaker, I always said yes to people because I enjoyed helping others. Although helping others is an important virtue, so is having boundaries. I realized that focusing on self-love and taking care of myself was very important. Having peace of mind, better health, and more stability comes first before I can attend to others. In order to become Her, I have to push myself and walk outside of my comfort zone. I must let go of anything that wastes my time and people not aligned with my values. Things that are not true to my purpose will not allow me to be free and will mess with my inner peace. So when I started becoming confident in who I am becoming, I started experiencing unspeakable joy from down within. Realizing that wanting to become doesn't mean that I am better than anyone; it means I want to be better today and from now on than yesterday. A better version of becoming her is not based on fear or disengagement from societal expectations or limitations. It is taking charge of my own life. I had to take charge and be accountable for my choices and decisions.

Working on me made me open up again to communicate and socialize with others. I was doing activities with my children and still working to find my happy place—a space of contentment with myself.

### I found Shawn again.

I am more persistent, fighting daily to become who I am destined to be and not letting any obstacles get in the way. I believe it is an act of self-awareness, self-love, self-security, and self-protection. It is a movement to show myself that each decision I make and every step that I take matters within me. I might even start to question the power from within. So, I promised myself that I am choosing right when I chose her (me). I want more out of life and choose not to give up on me. There will be no days off and no more room for excuses. It will take time and dedication, and I have to view myself as a work in progress. I have to do something every day to push forward to become. Stumbling blocks were and still may be along the way. But I've already decided to walk through them, around them, and do whatever is necessary to overcome them.

Although the old self can resist change, I have the ability to define who I want to be and then be that. And in doing so, I must understand the direction that I am heading and try my best to continue to aim toward becoming the best version of myself. Getting rid of the old and putting on the new is very important. I trust my own decisions. I am working on goals and doing things I enjoy to make things happen. "Becoming Her" has helped me become a better listener and understand people. During my journey, if there is anything about me that I want to improve, I have to look within and scripturally to the hills from where my help comes. Why? All of my help comes from the Lord. He made Heaven, Earth, and everything in between because I cannot do it by myself. I desire to live my best life, work on becoming Her for me, and not try to live up to anyone's standard.

I believe I am good, and he that finds a wife finds a good thing, and my husband found me. The crazy part, yet divine intervention of how this happened, stemmed from my attempt to socialize again. Attending one of my son's basketball games, and that's where my husband and I exchanged numbers. Our friendship started during our childhood days, but timing is everything.

If I had not made an effort to be back active and socializing, I would not have been able to meet my husband, Eddie. Eddie encouraged me a lot and helped me to understand there is more to life than just working. In school, you are taught to graduate, go to college, and work, but there's more. He's been so supportive of my growth. When I wanted to return to school for more education, he helped me get back to studying. I never thought I would be able to have a business, write my story and lead a different life, but thank God I have.

I've always taken care of people before gaining certification and after. Despite life circumstances, I became an elder in my church, a hospice specialist, and an honorable wife and mother. I am amazed at how it all started and how my life is now. I encourage younger people to know that life is more than what you see. Based on what I saw, I was going down the wrong path, but I discovered there is more to life than that.

We are never too old to stop learning, so I won't. My voice is worthy of being heard, and my opinion does matter. As I am still becoming, I am learning from my past mistakes and having a new mindset. "Becoming" implies being on your way toward something greater. Becoming Her meant understanding and unlocking my potential. It may sound like an inherently self-centered goal; however, it is an actual unselfish process. As I become Her, I recognize my powers, including being strong, confident, and competent. I understand my emotions and push towards what I want out of life. It will require a lot of work. It will require me to fight for my freedom and restoration. Hard work and consistency are necessary. I will not allow my past to ruin my future. Daily I am striving to become a better wife, a better mother, a better daughter, a better sister, a better niece, a better cousin, a better aunt, a better friend, and just an overall better person.

At one point, I struggled to know who I was and didn't know who I could be until I started understanding myself better. Building and maintaining a good relationship with God gave me joy, peace, kindness, temperance, patience, gentleness, and self-control in all areas of life. He empowered me more than I could have ever imagined. At first, I did not understand, but NOW I realize He had created me with everything I needed to "Become Her." I know there is a greater plan for me, my children, and my children's children.

Becoming starts with trusting in God. This means I must be true to myself and, more importantly, be faithful to Him. Going after the things He has for me, working hard to achieve them, and my refusal to give up has equipped me to remain steadfast. Looking back, I am fully committed to Becoming Her through the ups and downs: free, fulfilled, and purpose-driven.
As I close, I would like to share this prayer with you...

Almighty Father, thank you. Thank you for this opportunity to change. You know my heart's deep longings and what is best for me. Lord, help me as I desire to become. If it is your will, guide me. Lord, give me the wisdom and knowledge as you direct me. I'm not asking you to remove all obstacles that are in the way. I'm asking you to give me the strength to overcome them. Make the crooked paths straight and perfect everything. I pray that your peace and joy will always fill me when chaos and stress arise. I know you hold the key to my greatness in your hand, and may it ever be present in my life. Lord, keep filling my heart with your unspeakable joy. I hope I always find joy and contentment in you. I pray that you guard my heart and mind with the peace that only you can bring so that I will remain even when difficulties arise.

Thank you for loving me despite my imperfections. I pray that I can be loving and understanding just as you are. Please help me to extend grace toward others when needed and learn to pick my battles. As I come before you, God, I pray that my love will reflect respect, kindness, and trust. Please, Lord, remind me not to be self-centered and renew a better Her in me. Please help me to remember that becoming Her is more than a feeling, it is a choice. I pray that those who will read my story will be inspired, healed, and motivated to find their paths of Becoming! Be Blessed. Amen

# Dedication

I would like to dedicate this chapter to my Dad (Poppa G) with love.

Words cannot describe the appreciation that I have for you. You have always been my source of inspiration, support, and guidance. You have taught me to be unique, determined, and to believe that I can do anything I desire with the help of the Holy Spirit and to always persevere.

So I thank you for your love, wisdom and all the wonderful things you have done for me while you were here on this earth. You are truly missed.

*Your babygirl Shawn*

# REFLECTIONS

# REFLECTIONS

# Tamara Mitchell-Davis

## Deciding What's Best For Me

# Tamara Mitchell-Davis

## Deciding What's Best For Me

*"And we know that all things work together for good to them that love God, to them who are the called according to his purpose"*
*Romans 8:28*

In the realm of self-discovery, there comes a time when we must confront the daunting task of making tough decisions. Though necessary for our growth and fulfillment, these decisions may not always be favorable to those around us. Venturing down a path unknown, away from the expectations and desires of others, we begin to unravel the true essence of who we are and what life may be like when we become the best version of ourselves.

My journey of self-discovery led me to crossroads—an intersection where the desires of my heart collided with the expectations of those around me. For years, I had molded myself to fit the predetermined boxes that society, family and friends had crafted for me. I followed the path that seemed safe and secure, the one that promised stability and approval. Taking small risks, if any, because my focus was more on survival than risk-taking. Yet, deep within, I felt an undeniable yearning for something more that could not be contained within those confining boundaries.

As the weight pressed upon me, I found solace in a quiet corner of introspection. In that sacred space, I allowed myself to dream, to imagine a life beyond the confines of convention and people-pleasing. I understood that to be the best version of myself, a daring leap of faith was necessary, a willingness to embrace uncertainty and venture into uncharted territories.

The first step was acknowledging the tough decisions that awaited me. I knew that to honor my dreams and aspirations; I would have to disappoint and challenge the expectations of those around me. It was not an easy realization, for I had always sought approval and validation from others. The fear of disappointing them gnawed at me, but deep down; I eventually understood that my happiness and fulfillment could not be sacrificed for conformity.

This is no implication to those around me who loved me; it was the realization of what I did to seek love, acceptance, and approval yet still feeling empty.

Learning at an early age to treat others how I wanted to be treated seemed that I was often left with the short end of the stick. As a way to protect myself, I started creating boundaries and doing things that made me happy, which seemed to move me more into a corner of isolation. I was labeled as mean and only concerned about myself. This was furthest from the truth. I had always been consumed with everyone else's feelings and neglected my own. I wanted others to be happy and feel good at the expense of my happiness. It was a repeated cycle that I desperately wanted to break.

Venturing down the path less traveled is not without its challenges. It requires a resilience of spirit, a steadfast belief in one's abilities, and an unwavering commitment to personal growth. There were moments of self-doubt when the weight of uncertainty threatened to engulf me. As I embarked on this new journey, I realized that making sense of what life could potentially look like required a willingness to let go of preconceived notions and embrace the unknown. I embraced the discomfort of uncertainty, understanding that we truly discover our capabilities and resilience in those moments of vulnerability.

The path less traveled was not without its setbacks and obstacles. There were times when I stumbled and doubted my own choices. But with each setback, I learned invaluable lessons about myself and the world around me. I discovered my strength, ability to adapt, and capacity for resilience. I realized that societal standards did not solely define the measure of success but by the alignment of my actions with my deepest values and aspirations.

In the midst of the unknown, I found a sense of liberation. The shackles of others' expectations began to loosen, and I embraced the freedom to define my path. The choices I made were not always easy. But in honoring my own truth and pursuing the path that resonated with my soul, I discovered a profound sense of fulfillment and authenticity.

Life took on new colors as I ventured further down the path less traveled. It was not a linear journey but one filled with twists, turns, and surprises. Along the way, I met kindred spirits who understood the depths of my aspirations and supported me wholeheartedly. I also encountered individuals with hidden agendas. However, because I wholeheartedly believe that everything (good and bad) is always working for my greater good, these connections became pillars of strength, reminding me that I was not alone in my pursuit of becoming.

As I continued to navigate the unknown, I learned to embrace the beauty of uncertainty. I realized that life's greatest adventures often unfold when we release our need for control and allow ourselves to be guided by intuition and serendipity. Embracing the unknown meant relinquishing the safety net of predictability and stepping into the realm of possibility, where dreams had the space to manifest and flourish.

In the process, I found that making tough decisions that prioritize my growth and happiness didn't mean disregarding the feelings and needs of others. It meant finding a delicate balance between honoring my aspirations and maintaining compassion for those around me. As I pursued my journey, I learned the importance of open communication, empathy, and understanding in navigating relationships.

As I write today, reflecting upon the choices I have made and the path I have traveled, I am filled with a profound sense of gratitude. The tough decisions that weren't always favorable to others have shaped me into a person who is unafraid to follow her heart, who believes in the boundless potential within herself, and who embraces the unknown with unwavering courage.

Life has unfolded in ways I couldn't have imagined and probably would have never experienced if I decided that being stuck or feeling complacent was enough. Suppose I allowed the negative opinions of others to guide my actions. We all have our paths and journey in life. Each one of us has the ability to determine what BEcoming means. It meant, for me, acting in accordance with my highest ideals and principles. It meant embracing authenticity, self-love, and the unwavering belief that I am capable of creating a life that reflects my true essence.

As I continue forward, I am excited about what lies ahead. The unknown no longer holds fear but offers a playground for growth and exploration. We can decide to be victims of circumstances or victors of life. With each step we take, we move one step closer to becoming the person we feel we are meant to be, and that is a journey worth pursuing with every fiber of our being.

You have read stories of women who have made tough decisions, faced extenuating circumstances, ventured into the unknown, and embraced the path less traveled. Their experiences are a reflection of their journey, where they challenged societal expectations and discovered the boundless potential that lies within them. Their words will echo in your soul, resonating with your own experiences and reminding you of your own strength.

Mothers, daughters, sisters, friends, and strangers—who have walked paths both similar and vastly different from each other. However, the universal theme of love, loss, resilience, forgiveness, and hope is what abounds. Through their narratives, we find solace, inspiration, and the courage to confront our adversities, knowing we are not alone in our struggles.

I hope our stories will ignite a fire within you, urging you to confront your challenges with unwavering determination and resilience. No matter how insurmountable the obstacles may seem, there is always a flicker of hope waiting to be kindled within your heart. May the fire burn brighter than ever as you embrace the power of your story and remember you, too, have the strength to BEcome the woman you've always desired to be. Don't put it off any longer, BEcome Her Now!

# Dedication

This chapter is dedicated to the women who find themselves navigating the intricate web of life's choices, often faced with unsolicited opinions and raised eyebrows.

May you experience freedom from the chains of guilt and find the strength to prioritize your own well being.

# REFLECTIONS

_____
_____
_____
_____
_____
_____
_____
_____
_____
_____
_____
_____
_____
_____
_____
_____
_____
_____
_____
_____

# REFLECTIONS

_____

_____

_____

_____

_____

_____

_____

_____

_____

_____

_____

_____

_____

_____

_____

_____

_____

_____

# REFLECTIONS

# JOURNAL
## PROMPTS

# Which Chapter resonated with you the most and Why?

_____

_____

_____

_____

_____

_____

_____

_____

_____

_____

_____

_____

_____

_____

_____

What areas can you identify as opportunities for growth to BEcome the person you've always desired to be in spite of situations and circumstances?

_____

_____

_____

_____

_____

_____

_____

_____

_____

_____

_____

_____

# What practice or goal(s) can you set for yourself to put you on the path you desire?

_____

_____

_____

_____

_____

_____

_____

_____

_____

_____

_____

_____

_____

_____

_____

_____

# What kind of support(s) or resources do you need for change?

_____

_____

_____

_____

_____

_____

_____

_____

_____

_____

_____

_____

_____

# What would be your evidence of progress?

_____

_____

_____

_____

_____

_____

_____

_____

_____

_____

_____

_____

_____

How would Becoming make you feel once you've arrived? Be sure to hold that feeling close to your heart and each day move in the direction you wish to go in order to BEcome her now!

_____

_____

_____

_____

_____

_____

_____

_____

_____

_____

_____

_____

_____

_____

_____

_____

# Becoming Her

## BONUS

Becoming the best version of oneself will look different for each and every person who desires to do the work, internally and externally. Work that includes a path to self-improvement, self-reflection, self-discovery and personal growth with the goal of gaining a better and deeper understanding of who you are, your values, passions, and aspirations. When you seek change, here's what can happen:

**Clarity and Direction:** You can create a roadmap to follow, helping you set meaningful goals, make informed decisions, and stay focused on your path.

**Self-Discovery:** You can uncover your true potential and purpose in life.

**Empowerment:** Shifting your mindset to take control of your life to move from being a passive observer to an active participant in shaping your own destiny.

**Resilience and Growth:** Overcoming challenges, embracing failure, and learning from setbacks builds resilience, adaptability, and a growth mindset, enabling you to bounce back stronger and grow from experiences.

**Fulfillment and Happiness:** Be intentional to align your actions and choices with your true self to experience a greater sense of fulfillment and happiness that brings you joy and satisfaction.

**Positive Impact on Others:** Inspire and positively impact others around you. Your growth and personal development can serve as an example and catalyst for change in the lives of those you interact with.

The journey of becoming is not a destination but a lifelong process. It encourages continuous learning, allowing you to evolve and adapt to new challenges and opportunities.

1. Begin by taking some time for self-reflection. Ask yourself, "Who am I? Who do I want to become?" Consider your values, strengths, and aspirations. This introspective process will lay the foundation for your journey.

2. Evaluate your current state of being in different areas of your life—such as relationships, career, health, and personal development. Identify areas where you feel there is room for improvement and growth.

3. Keep a journal or record your progress along the way. Celebrate your achievements, note any insights, and reflect on how each step is shaping your growth. Tracking your progress will help you stay motivated and provide a reference point for reflection.

4. Surround yourself with a supportive community. Share your journey with like-minded individuals, seek guidance from mentors, or consider joining accountability groups. Collaboration and support from others can greatly enhance your growth process.

Remember, small consistent steps create lasting change. Your journey is personal, and customization will ensure a more meaningful and fulfilling experience.

Here's a few ways to start exploring your path to **B.E.C.O.M.E** the person you've always desired to be. Try one, a few or all.

# **B**: Believe in Yourself:

Identify and acknowledge your unique strengths, talents, and skills. Focus on what you excel at and take pride in your accomplishments. Reflect on past achievements to boost your confidence. This can be your personal brag area!

_____

_____

_____

_____

_____

_____

_____

_____

_____

_____

_____

_____

_____

# E: Explore Your Passions

If you are feeling stuck or wondering what your purpose is, be open to exploring your passions and interests. You'd be surprised what new ideas, or opportunities open up for you once you take action and start moving toward it. List your passions.

_____

_____

_____

_____

_____

_____

What have you been interested in, considered doing but never took the time to read about, try or experience?

_____

_____

_____

_____

_____

What would be a next step for you, once you have identified it or them? What do you need to set up? Who do you need to call? What do you need to schedule?

_____

_____

_____

_____

_____

_____

_____

_____

Step out of your comfort zone and engage in activities that challenge you in order to help you build resilience and confidence. Start with small, manageable steps and gradually increase the level of difficulty.

_____

_____

_____

_____

_____

_____

_____

_____

# C: Communication

Develop the ability to articulate your thoughts, ideas, and emotions effectively. Use clear and concise language, organize your thoughts beforehand, and consider the needs and background of your audience.

1. Practice nonverbal communication: Pay attention to your nonverbal cues, such as body language, facial expressions, and tone of voice. Ensure that your nonverbal signals align with your verbal message to enhance understanding and avoid misinterpretation.

2. Practice active listening and seek to understand different perspectives.

3. Practice positive self-talk: Replace self-doubt and negative thoughts with positive affirmations and self-talk. Remind yourself of your capabilities, strengths, and past successes. Visualize yourself achieving your goals and embodying confidence.

_____

_____

_____

_____

_____

_____

_____

_____

# O: Overcome Obstacles

An obstacle is an opportunity for growth and learning. By approaching challenges with a positive mindset, strategic planning, and perseverance, you can overcome obstacles and continue moving forward on your path to becoming the best version of yourself.

1. Take a step back and objectively evaluate the obstacle. Understand its nature, scope, and potential impact on your goals. Break it down into smaller, manageable parts to make it less daunting.

2. Develop a positive and resilient mindset that sees obstacles as opportunities for growth. Embrace the belief that you have the ability to overcome challenges and find solutions.

3. Define specific goals that you want to achieve despite the obstacle. Clear goals provide direction and motivation, keeping you focused on finding solutions rather than getting overwhelmed by the obstacle.

4. Reach out to supportive individuals, such as friends, family, mentors, or colleagues. Share your obstacle(s) and seek their advice, perspective, or assistance. Collaborating with others can provide new insights and support to help overcome the obstacle.

5. Create a strategic plan to address the obstacle. Outline the specific actions, resources, and timelines needed to overcome it. A well-thought-out plan helps you stay organized and focused on the steps required for success.

6. Start taking action towards overcoming the obstacle. Begin with the first step and build momentum as you make progress. Consistent action is key to breaking through barriers.

7. Maintain your motivation and persistence throughout the process. Remind yourself of your goals, visualize the desired outcome, and celebrate small victories along the way. Keep pushing forward, even when faced with adversity.
.

# M: Motivate and Inspire

Stay motivated by envisioning your desired future. Keep your eyes on your prize.

# E: Evolve and Keep Learning

1. Embrace a growth mindset and continually seek personal development.

2. Be open to learning from experiences, books, courses, and mentors.

You cannot change the past but you are well equipped to change the trajectory of your desired future.

# MEET THE
## AUTHORS

# Shakeasha Shelby

Shakeasha Shelby, a native of Los Angeles, California, is a talented and passionate hair stylist, entrepreneur, and mentor. Having grown up in San Bernardino County, she pursued her dreams by attending Beauty School and honing her skills in hairstyling. Today, Shakeasha is the proud founder and owner of "Beautifully Collected", a thriving business that has earned her recognition such as creating stunning, cohesive hairstyles for the Grammy's 2023 performers.

With specialized braiding and permanent makeup certifications, Shakeasha's expertise goes beyond hairstyling. She is dedicated to providing guidance on promoting hair growth and building confidence through a healthier self-care routine.

Passionate about empowering young black and brown girls, Shakeasha has refocused her vision to help them realize their entrepreneurial aspirations. Through her mentorship, she encourages young girls to elevate their minds and embrace their limitless potential. Shakeasha believes in instilling self-esteem and confidence within young girls, showing them that they have been empowered to transform their gifts into successful businesses. She strives to empower them to become leaders and bosses in their own right, inspiring future generations of entrepreneurs. With her expertise and unwavering commitment, Shakeasha Shelby is making a lasting impact on the lives of aspiring young entrepreneurs.

You can connect with Shakeasha at:

✉ ShakeashaShelby@gmail.com

📷 Beautifully_Collected

# Dr. Lashonda Wofford

Dr. Lashonda Wofford founded and built several successful organizations, including an affirmation collection, L&S Consulting Group: I Am Mrs. Lashonda Wofford, LLC dba All Bets On Me, and Wofford & Williams Inc. d/b/a Akins Helping Hands.

She is a community advocate and personal development partner who encourages all to bet on themselves through her All Bets on Me platform on Facebook. Dr. Wofford has learned to bet on herself and accomplish her goals despite adversities through various pains and struggles. She holds a PhD in Christian Education and is a successful businesswoman of color who breaks the ceiling and creates tables for other women to have the same opportunities as she has.

Some of Dr. Wofford's noteworthy accomplishments include serving in the following roles: accredited certified instructor for Purpose Zeal Academy, certified executive leadership coach, certified life recovery coach, certified mental health counselor and certified transformational coach. She is a five-time best-selling author and the recipient of the 2022 ACHI Award for Public Service. Her books include anthology projects: Blessed Not Broken, Vol. I; Igniting Your Purpose; 90 Days of Biblical Affirmations for Christian Women in Business and Ministry; Love Business Marriage and her solo project Pain Equals Purpose, all of which can be purchased on her website.

Dr. Wofford is a proud member of Sigma Tau Sigma Sorority, and she strives to live out God's plans for her life as she engages with others. She enjoys spending time with her family (especially her grandchildren), relaxing, reading, and practicing good self-care habits in her spare time. She resides in North Carolina with her husband and their family.

You can connect with Dr. Wofford:

🌐 www.mrslashondawofford.com.

👤 Dr.LashondaWofford

👤 All Bets On Me

👤 All Things Coaching Community

# Celeste Dowdell

Celeste Dowdell is a serial entrepreneur. She is the CEO of NuAttitude by Celeste and serves as an independent agent with InteleTravel. She is an independent consultant for Traveling Vineyard and has worked with the State of Connecticut for nearly two decades in the practitioner licensing department.

In addition to her career and running multiple businesses, Celeste is a founding member and Vice President of Connecticut's first chapter of Theta Alpha Sigma Philo Affiliate for Sigma Gamma Rho Sorority, Inc. She is also currently enrolled at Southern New Hampshire University, pursuing her Bachelor's degree in Business Administration with a concentration in Entrepreneurship.

Celeste is the mother of three amazing young men, grandmother to one adorable grandson, and one fur baby. She loves to work out at the gym, travel, sing karaoke, try new types of food, and spend time with family and friends. Celeste currently resides in Connecticut with her family.

You can connect with Celeste at:

✉ celestedowdell@yahoo.com

f Celeste Dowdell

⊚ nuattitudeby_celeste

# Jacquelyn Santiago Nazario

Jacquelyn Santiago Nazario is the Chief Executive Officer of COMPASS Youth Collaborative and a Human Relations Commissioner for the City of Hartford. She is a champion for youth equity, a dynamic youth development trainer, and an advocate for youths living at risk. Jackie obtained her Bachelor's degree in Sociology from Trinity College in 2000 and her Master's degree from Quinnipiac University's School of Business in 2014. She is a national trainer in youth development practices and the seven executive functions of the brain.

Jackie currently serves on the Commission on Gun Violence Prevention and Intervention appointed by Speaker of the House Matt Ritter and sits on the Governor's Workforce Council on Youth Diversity, Equity, and Inclusion. She advocates for and creates awareness about the best practices for working with youths impacted by the juvenile justice system and violence. A native of Lawrence, MA, Jackie had early experiences as many of the young people who inspire her today. She decided in high school that if she were lucky enough to go to college, she would do something to help children and their families succeed. She believes all youth will thrive when given the needed resources and opportunities to do so.

Jackie was named one of Hartford Business Journal's 40 under 40 in 2015 and 100 Women of Color in 2017. Other recognitions include Hartford's Champion for Youth and Leadership Development award in 2018, the Urban League of Greater Hartford's Champion of Justice Award in 2019, Trinity College's 50 for the Next 50 Award, and the 2023 Latina Champion

Award. Jackie is a loving mother of 1 biological child, two bonus children whom she loves like her own and a wife to her adoring husband, Iran Nazario.

You can connect with Jaquelyn at:

✉ JackieNazarioMotivation@gmail.com

ⓕ Jacquelyn Santiago Nazario

📷 nazario__jacquelyn

in Jacquelyn Santiago Nazario

# Ann-Gela Holloway

Ann-Gela Holloway is an author, coach, poet, speaker and actress. She holds Business degrees from Albertus Magnus College in New Haven, CT. She has had a twenty-year-long career with the State of Connecticut and is currently employed at the Department of Mental Health and Addiction Services, where she serves as a Business Manager.

In 2021, ACHI magazine nominated Ann-Gela as Author of the Year! In that same year, she was featured in Voyage MIA magazine. She has been a guest on radio shows and podcasts throughout the nation. Ann-Gela is a mom to two sons and reside in her home state of Connecticut. She enjoys traveling, especially visiting new states, hoping to set foot in all 50 one day.

Her first solo book project, "Let Me Tell You What I Know," is available on Amazon.

You can connect with Ann-Gela at:

 anngela.holloway

# Shawn Goines-Rozetta

Shawn Goines-Rozetta is a servant and disciple of Jesus Christ and an oracle of the Lord through the gospel. She serves as the second vice-president of United Holy Church of America (UHCA) New England district missionary ministry and as president of Ebenezer Temple Missionaries. She co-founded and hosts the Facebook live stream: "About Our Father's Business!" to share spiritual downloads and inspiration at a time when she and her husband were navigating rough waters themselves.

Shawn works as a hospice specialist and obtained her Bachelor's degree in theology from United Christian College. She is also certified as a medical assistant and parent coach.

Shawn is the mother of five and grandmother of three. She enjoys volunteering at local senior facilities and traveling with her husband, Elder Eddie Rozetta, who is also a singer. They reside in Connecticut with their family.

You can connect with Shawn at:

✉ ShawniegProductions@gmail.com

✉ shawngoinesrozetta@gmail.com

f Shawn Goines-Rozetta

⬚ Shawn Goines-Rozetta

# Tamara Mitchell-Davis

Tamara Mitchell-Davis is a multi-bestselling and award-winning author. She is the CEO of TM Davis Enterprise, LLC, a dynamic training and development company that empowers aspiring authors, thought leaders, and entrepreneurs to bring their BOOK AND BUSINESS visions to life.

Tamara holds a Master's degree in Business Administration and an 085 School Business Administrator Certification from the State of Connecticut. Her published works include #GoalGetter: Strategies for Overcoming Life's Challenges; Goodbye Fear, Hello Destiny; Dream Your Plan, Plan Your Dream: 7 Steps to Manifesting Success; Blessed Not Broken (Vols.1, 2, 3, 4 and 5), Love Business & Marriage and coauthor in Dear Momma.

She is the founder of Pen to Profit: Write, Publish & Build community on Facebook, the host of the annual Pen to Profit Conference for authors, speakers and coaches, and the creator and host of The CEO Wife Experience Podcast.

Tamara's awards include: 100 Women of Color for leadership and community service; ACHI Magazine Orator of the Year; Women of Elevation Triumphant Author; I Am H.E.R International Woman on the Rise and CEO of the Year; and Phenomenal Woman In Business, to name a few.

Media appearances include Women of Distinction Magazine, Inquiring News, Making Headline News, Voyage Dallas Magazine, Voyage ATL Magazine, CanvasRebel and Black Women Mean Business Magazine.

She is an active member of Delta Sigma Theta Sorority, Incorporated, and resides in Connecticut with her husband and their children.

You can connect with Tamara at

✉ info@theceowife.com,

🌐 www.theceowife.com.

f theceowife

📷 theceowife860

# NEVER STOP LEARNING

---

# NEVER STOP DREAMING!

## NEVER STOP EVOLVING TO BECOME THE PERSON WHO GOD CREATED YOU TO BE!

Printed in the USA
CPSIA information can be obtained
at www.ICGtesting.com
JSHW060004160823
46589JS00003B/22